Contents

La maison

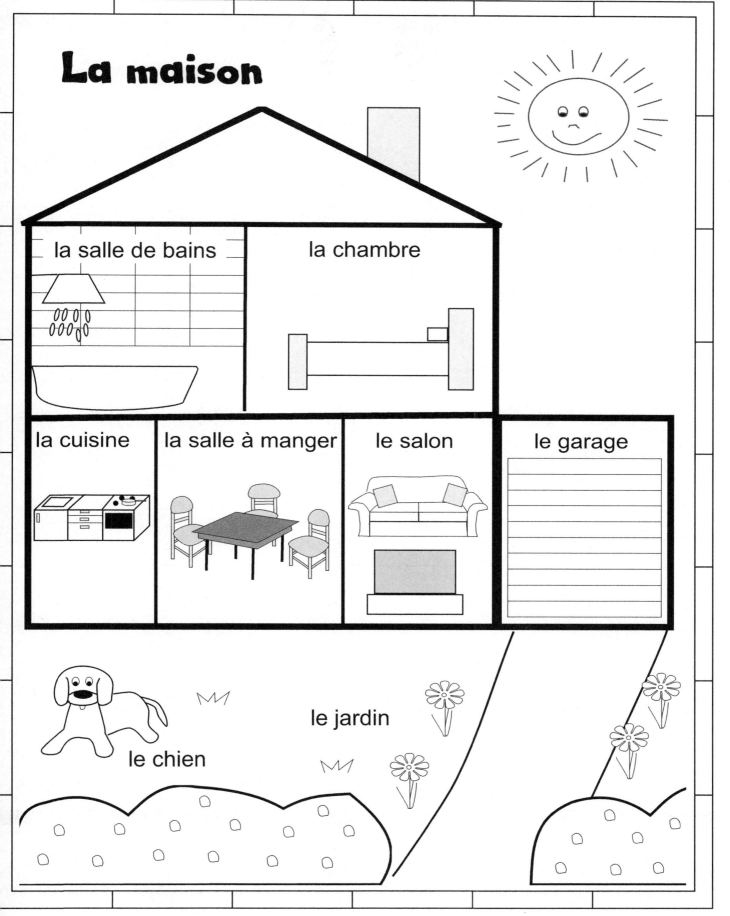

la salle de bains

la chambre

la cuisine

la salle à manger

le salon

le garage

le jardin

le chien

1

Qu'est-ce que c'est? (What is it?)

Écrire les mots en français: (Write the words in French:)

1)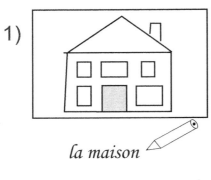

la maison

2)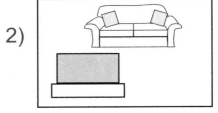

_____

3)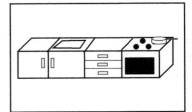

_____

4)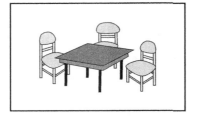

_____

5)

_____

6)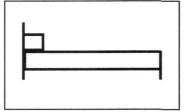

_____

7)

_____

 le salon   le jardin   la cuisine   la maison   la chambre   la salle à manger   la salle de bain

C'est de quelle couleur? (What colour is it?)

bleu.......... blue

vert ....green

rouge ....red

violet......... purple

marron ..... brown

rose .... pink

et .... and

Colorier en utilisant les bonnes couleurs:

La cuisine est rouge.

La salle à manger est marron et rose.

Le salon est violet.

La salle de bains est bleue.

La chambre principale est verte.

La petite chambre est rose.

Notice how in the sentences above vert has changed to verte, and bleu to bleue. This has happened because the colours are describing a feminine noun.

le salon   la cuisine   la chambre principale   la petite chambre   la salle à manger   la salle de bains

                        (the main bedroom)   (the small bedroom)

Language detective time!

Have you noticed that in French sometimes the words start with le, la, un or une? Do you know why this is? Well in French, nouns are either masculine (boy words) or feminine (girl words), and because of this there is more than one way of saying **the** and **a**.

For a singular masculine noun, the is **le**, and a is **un**. For masculine nouns beginning with a vowel, le is shortened to l'.

For a singular feminine noun, the is **la**, and a is **une**. For example,
La salle de bains = the bathroom   Une salle de bains = a bathroom

1) Compléter le tableau. (Complete the table:)

Masculine words	
le = the un = a	
The	a
le jardin	*un* jardin
le salon	___ salon
___ garage	un garage

Feminine words	
la = the une = a	
The	a
la maison	*une* maison
___ cuisine	une cuisine
la chambre	___ chambre

2) C'est masculin ou féminin? (Is it masculine or feminine?)

a) la salle à manger   *feminine* _____

b) le salon   _____

c) la salle de bains   _____

4

Où sont les animaux? (Where are the pets?)

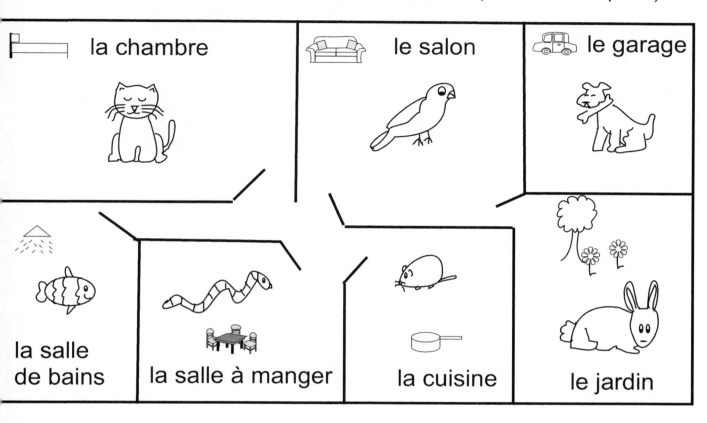

Sophie a beaucoup d'animaux. (Sophie has a lot of pets.)

Répondre aux questions: (Answer the questions:)

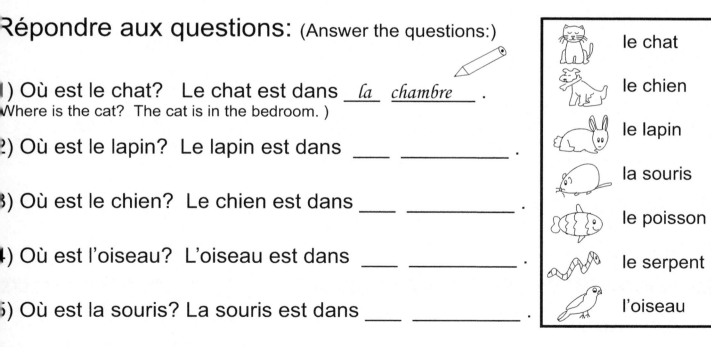

1) Où est le chat?   Le chat est dans _la chambre_ .
Where is the cat? The cat is in the bedroom.)

2) Où est le lapin? Le lapin est dans ___ _____ .

3) Où est le chien? Le chien est dans ___ _____ .

4) Où est l'oiseau? L'oiseau est dans ___ _____ .

5) Où est la souris? La souris est dans ___ _____ .

6) Où est le poisson? Le poisson est dans ___ _____ ___ _____ .

7) Où est le serpent? Le serpent est dans ___ _____ ___ _____ .

Maisons à vendre (Houses for sale)

A

Il y a un salon, une cuisine, une salle à manger, trois chambres et une salle de bains.

B

Il y a une cuisine, un salon, un jardin, une salle de bains et deux chambres.

C

Il y a un salon, une cuisine, une salle de bains, quatre chambres et un garage.

Lire les descriptions. (Read the descriptions)
C'est quelle maison? (Which house is it?)

B

1) There are two bedrooms. _____

2) There are three bedrooms. _____

3) There are four bedrooms. _____

4) There is a dining room. _____

5) There is a garden. _____

6) There is a garage. _____

un salon	une cuisine	Il y a = there is / are
un jardin	une salle à manger	deux chambres = two bedrooms
		trois chambres = three bedrooms
un garage	une salle de bains	quatre chambres = four bedrooms

La maison (the house)

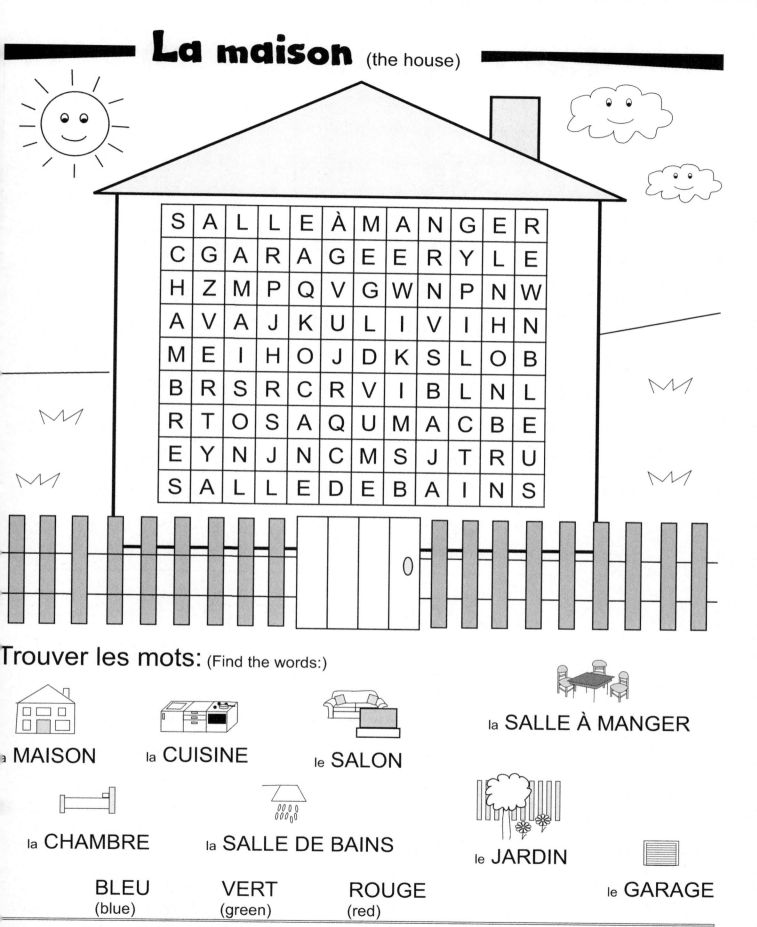

S	A	L	L	E	À	M	A	N	G	E	R
C	G	A	R	A	G	E	E	R	Y	L	E
H	Z	M	P	Q	V	G	W	N	P	N	W
A	V	A	J	K	U	L	I	V	I	H	N
M	E	I	H	O	J	D	K	S	L	O	B
B	R	S	R	C	R	V	I	B	L	N	L
R	T	O	S	A	Q	U	M	A	C	B	E
E	Y	N	J	N	C	M	S	J	T	R	U
S	A	L	L	E	D	E	B	A	I	N	S

Trouver les mots: (Find the words:)

la MAISON

la CUISINE

le SALON

la SALLE À MANGER

la CHAMBRE

la SALLE DE BAINS

le JARDIN

le GARAGE

BLEU
(blue)

VERT
(green)

ROUGE
(red)

In French there are four different ways of saying our word "the" : le, l', la, les.
These words do not appear in the word search.

7

Les numéros 21 - 30

30 trente

29 vingt-neuf

28 vingt-huit

27 vingt-sept

26 vingt-six

25 vingt-cinq

24 vingt-quatre

23 vingt-trois

22 vingt-deux

21 vingt-et-un

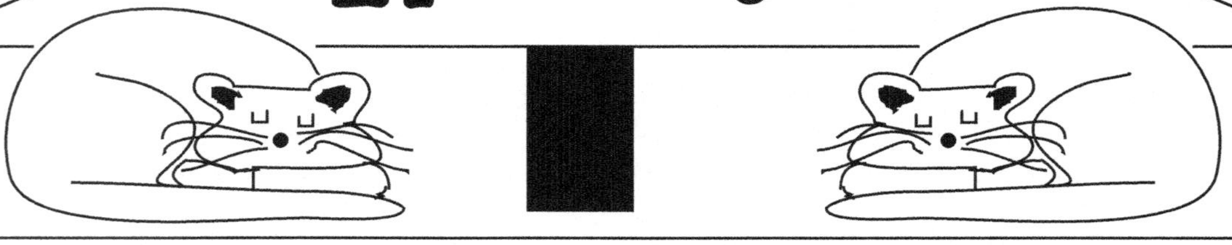

Les numéros 21 - 30

Relier les numéros aux mots. (Match the numbers to the words.)

24

vingt-deux

26

29

vingt-quatre

vingt-six

vingt-et-un

21

22

vingt-trois

vingt-neuf

23

28

vingt-cinq

Have you noticed that for the numbers 21 to 29 one of the numbers has an extra word in the French?

21 in French has the word "et" in between the two French numbers but the other numbers from 22 to 29 don't.

vingt-huit

25

21	22	23	24	25	26	27	28	29	30
ngt-et-un	vingt-deux	vingt-trois	vingt-quatre	vingt-cinq	vingt-six	vingt-sept	vingt-huit	vingt-neuf	trente

Les numéros 21 - 30

C'est quel numéro? Écrire le mot en français.
(What number is it? Write the word in French.)

a) **27** *vingt-sept*

b) **24**

c) **22**

d) **25**

e) **28**

f) **29**

g) **21**

h) **30**

21	**22**	**23**	**24**	**25**	**26**	**27**	**28**	**29**	**30**
vingt-et-un	vingt-deux	vingt-trois	vingt-quatre	vingt-cinq	vingt-six	vingt-sept	vingt-huit	vingt-neuf	tren

Les numéros 31 - 40

11

C'est quel numéro? (What number is it?)

C'est quel numéro? Écrire le mot en français.
(What number is it? Write the word in French.)

a)

trente-deux

_____

b)

_____

c)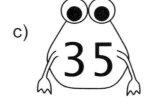

_____

d)

_____

e)

_____

f) 40

_____

g) 31

_____

h) 39

_____

31	32	33	34	35	36	37	38	39	40
trente-et-un	trente-deux	trente-trois	trente-quatre	trente-cinq	trente-six	trente-sept	trente-huit	trente-neuf	quaran

Les maths

Faire les calculs: (Do the calculations:)

Écrire les résultats en français: (Write the answers in French)

a) quatre x un = _____*quatre*_____

b) quatre x deux = _____

c) quatre x trois = _____

d) quatre x quatre = _____

e) quatre x cinq = _____

f) quatre x six = _____

g) quatre x sept = _____

h) quatre x huit = _____

i) quatre x neuf = _____

j) quatre x dix = _____

1 un	11 onze	21 vingt-et-un	31 trente-et-un
2 deux	12 douze	22 vingt-deux	32 trente-deux
3 trois	13 treize	23 vingt-trois	33 trente-trois
4 quatre	14 quatorze	24 vingt-quatre	34 trente-quatre
5 cinq	15 quinze	25 vingt-cinq	35 trente-cinq
6 six	16 seize	26 vingt-six	36 trente-six
7 sept	17 dix-sept	27 vingt-sept	37 trente-sept
8 huit	18 dix-huit	28 vingt-huit	38 trente-huit
9 neuf	19 dix-neuf	29 vingt-neuf	39 trente-neuf
10 dix	20 vingt	30 trente	40 quarante

13

Les numéros 21-40

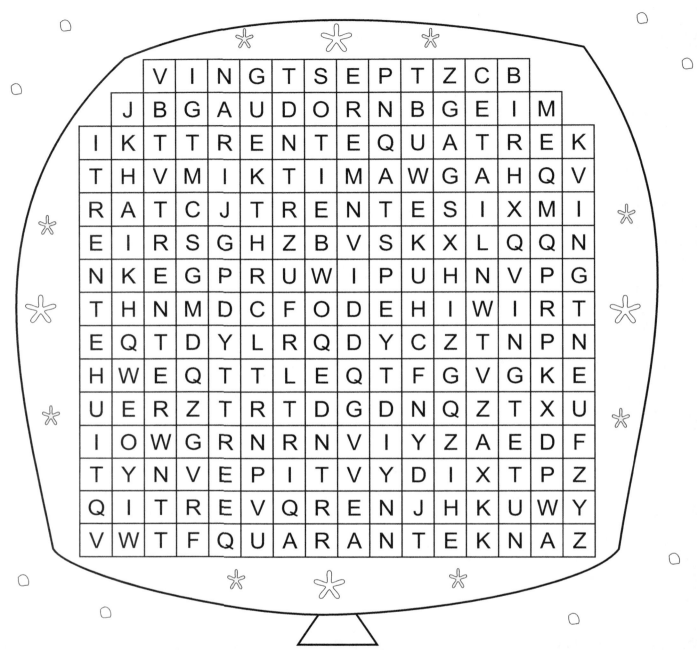

V	I	N	G	T	S	E	P	T	Z	C	B
J	B	G	A	U	D	O	R	N	B	G	E	I	M
I	K	T	T	R	E	N	T	E	Q	U	A	T	R	E	K
T	H	V	M	I	K	T	I	M	A	W	G	A	H	Q	V
R	A	T	C	J	T	R	E	N	T	E	S	I	X	M	I
E	I	R	S	G	H	Z	B	V	S	K	X	L	Q	Q	N
N	K	E	G	P	R	U	W	I	P	U	H	N	V	P	G
T	H	N	M	D	C	F	O	D	E	H	I	W	I	R	T
E	Q	T	D	Y	L	R	Q	D	Y	C	Z	T	N	P	N
H	W	E	Q	T	T	L	E	Q	T	F	G	V	G	K	E
U	E	R	Z	T	R	T	D	G	D	N	Q	Z	T	X	U
I	O	W	G	R	N	R	N	V	I	Y	Z	A	E	D	F
T	Y	N	V	E	P	I	T	V	Y	D	I	X	T	P	Z
Q	I	T	R	E	V	Q	R	E	N	J	H	K	U	W	Y
V	W	T	F	Q	U	A	R	A	N	T	E	K	N	A	Z

Trouver ces mots: (Look for these words:)

10	**20**	**21**	**23**	**25**
DIX	VINGT	VINGT-ET-UN	VINGT-TROIS	VINGT-CINQ

27	**29**	**30**	**32**
VINGT-SEPT	VINGT-NEUF	TRENTE	TRENTE-DEUX

34	**36**	**38**	**40**
TRENTE-QUATRE	TRENTE-SIX	TRENTE-HUIT	QUARANTE

La ville

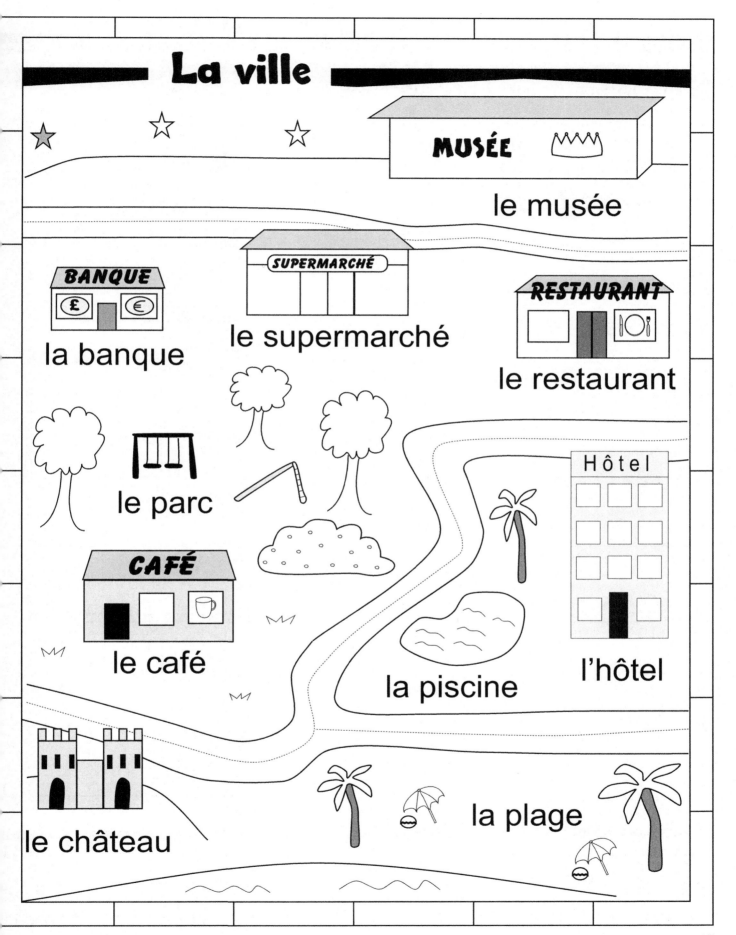

le musée

la banque

le supermarché

le restaurant

le parc

le café

la piscine

l'hôtel

le château

la plage

Qu'est-ce que c'est? (What is it?)

Écrire les mots en français: (Write the words in French:)

1)

le château ✎

_____

2)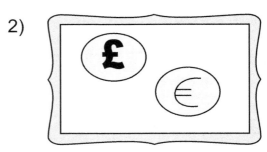

_____

3)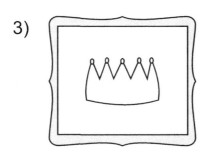

_____

4)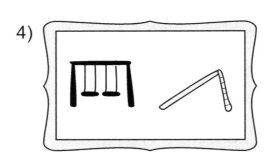

_____

5)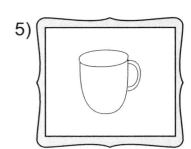

_____

6)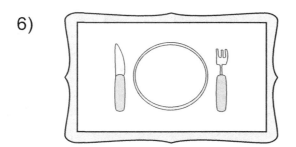

_____

7)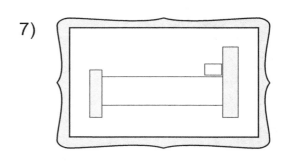

_____

 le château le parc le musée le café le restaurant l'hôtel la banque

Qu'est-ce qu'il y a? (What is there?)

| Dans ma ville - - In my town | il y a ✓ - - - there is | et - and |

| ✗ il n'y a pas de - - - there isn't | After il n'y a pas de you don't need le or la. |

Remplacer les dessins avec le bon mot:
Replace the pictures with the correct word:)

la plage

Dans ma ville il y a __ _____ et __ _____ .

Il y a __ _____ .

Il y a __ _____ et __ _____ .

✓

__ ____ __ le supermarché et __ _____ .

Il n'y a pas de _____ . Il n'y a pas de _____ .

le parc | le café | le restaurant | la banque | la piscine | la plage | musée | château

17

Ma ville (my town)

Salut,

Dans ma ville il y a le musée. J'aime le musée, c'est grand.

Il n'y a pas de plage.

Il y a le supermarché. Je n'aime pas le supermarché. C'est petit.

Il y a la piscine. J'aime la piscine.

Il n'y a pas de banque.

Il y a l'hôtel. C'est petit.

Salut!   *Sophie*

Salut - - - - - - - - -	Hi / Bye
Dans ma ville - - -	In my town
il y a - - - - - - - - -	there is
il n'y a pas de - - -	there isn't
J'aime - - - - - - - -	I like
Je n'aime pas - -	I don't like
C'est grand - - - -	it's big
C'est petit - - - - -	it' small

Lire la lettre de Sophie et répondre aux questions:
(Read the letter from Sophie and answer the questions)

Yes

1) Does Sophie like the museum in her town? _____

2) Is the museum big or small? _____

3) Is there a beach? _____

4) Does Sophie like the supermarket? _____

5) Is the supermarket big or small? _____

6) Is there a swimming pool? _____

7) Is there a bank? _____

8) Is the hotel big or small? _____

 le musée

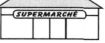 le supermarché

 l'hôtel

 la banque

 la plage

 la piscine

Language detective time!

Do you remember why French words sometimes start with le, la, un or une? Well in French, nouns are either masculine (boy words) or feminine (girl words), and because of this there is more than one way of saying our word **the** and our word **a**.

For singular masculine nouns, the is **le**, and a is **un**.

For singular feminine nouns, the is **la**, and a is **une**.

For example, le musée = the museum   un musée = a museum

1) Compléter le tableau. (Complete the table:)

Masculine words		**Feminine words**	
le = the	**un = a**	**la = the**	**une = a**
The	a	The	a
le musée	*un* musée	la banque	*une* banque
__ restaurant	un restaurant	____ plage	une plage
le château	____ château	la piscine	____ piscine
le parc	____ parc		
____ café	un café		

2) For l'hôtel the word **le** is shortened to **l'** because hôtel starts with the letter h and le often shortened to l' for nouns beginning with h. L'hôtel means the hotel.

a) What does un hôtel mean?   _____

b) Is un hôtel a masculine or a feminine word?   _____

19

Un peu de grammaire (a little grammar)

Relier les mots français aux mots anglais:
(Match the French words to the English words.)

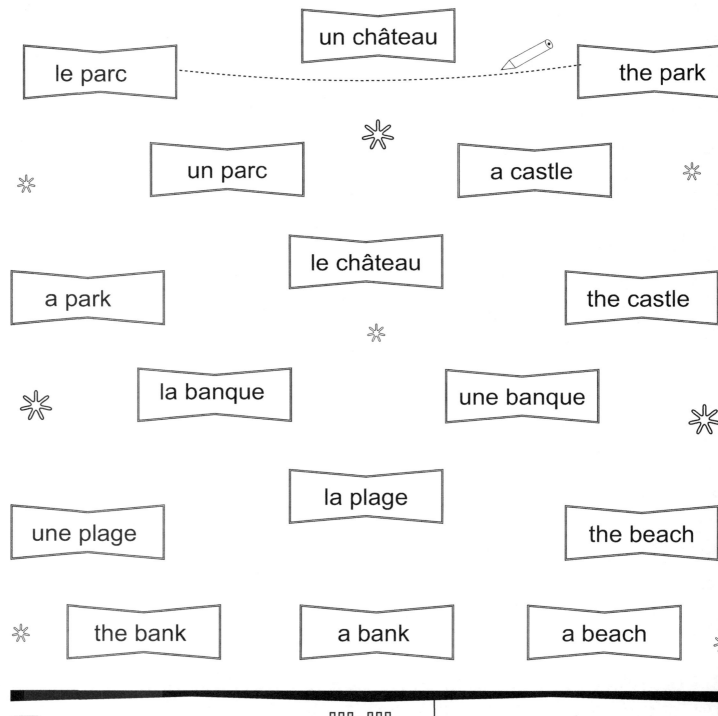

un château

le parc ········· the park

un parc

a castle

le château

a park

the castle

la banque

une banque

la plage

une plage

the beach

the bank

a bank

a beach

---

parc

banque

plage

château

un and une both mean "a"

le and la both mean "the"

La ville (the town / city)

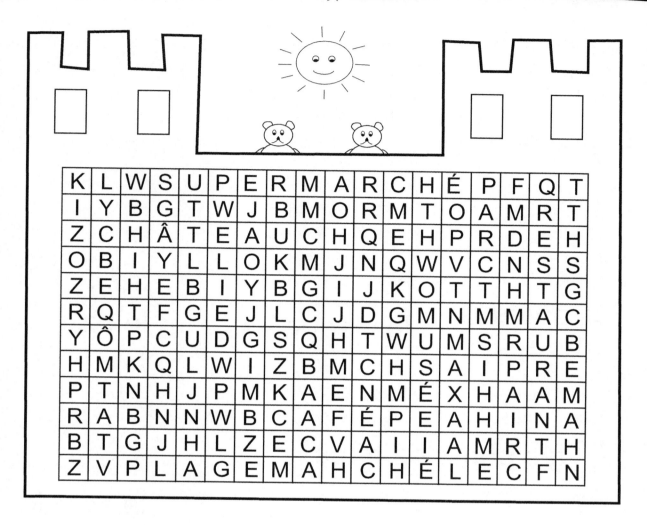

K	L	W	S	U	P	E	R	M	A	R	C	H	É	P	F	Q	T
I	Y	B	G	T	W	J	B	M	O	R	M	T	O	A	M	R	T
Z	C	H	Â	T	E	A	U	C	H	Q	E	H	P	R	D	E	H
O	B	I	Y	L	L	O	K	M	J	N	Q	W	V	C	N	S	S
Z	E	H	E	B	I	Y	B	G	I	J	K	O	T	T	H	T	G
R	Q	T	F	G	E	J	L	C	J	D	G	M	N	M	M	A	C
Y	Ô	P	C	U	D	G	S	Q	H	T	W	U	M	S	R	U	B
H	M	K	Q	L	W	I	Z	B	M	C	H	S	A	I	P	R	E
P	T	N	H	J	P	M	K	A	E	N	M	É	X	H	A	A	M
R	A	B	N	N	W	B	C	A	F	É	P	E	A	H	I	N	A
B	T	G	J	H	L	Z	E	C	V	A	I	I	A	M	R	T	H
Z	V	P	L	A	G	E	M	A	H	C	H	É	L	E	C	F	N

Trouver les mots: (Find the words:)

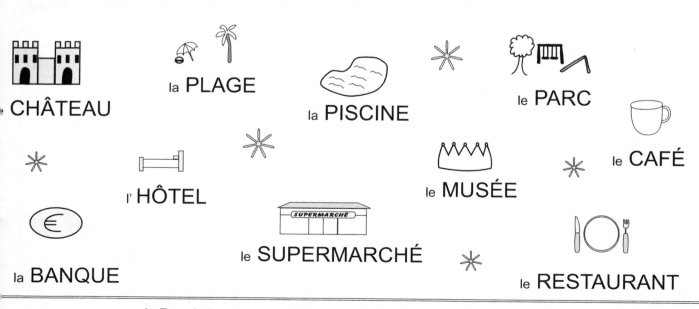

CHÂTEAU

la PLAGE

la PISCINE

le PARC

le CAFÉ

l' HÔTEL

le MUSÉE

le SUPERMARCHÉ

la BANQUE

le RESTAURANT

In French there are four different ways of saying our word "the" : le, l', la, les.
These words do not appear in the word search.

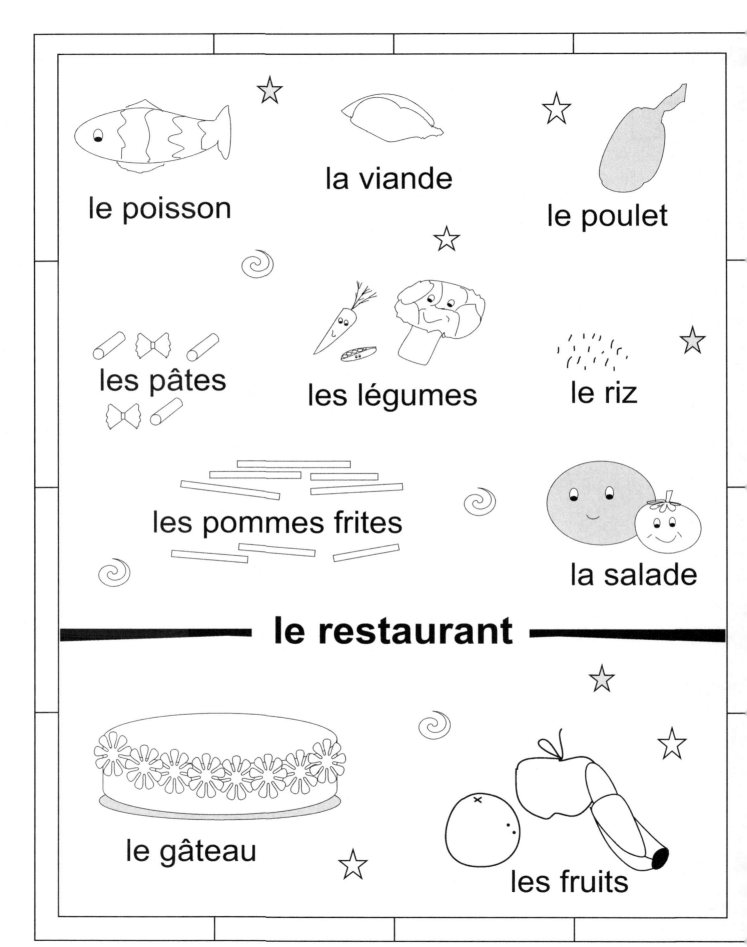

le poisson

la viande

le poulet

les pâtes

les légumes

le riz

les pommes frites

la salade

le restaurant

le gâteau

les fruits

Qu'est-ce que c'est? (What is it?)

Écrire les mots en français: (Write the words in French:)

1)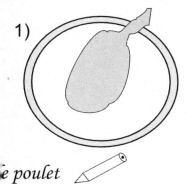

e poulet ✏️

2)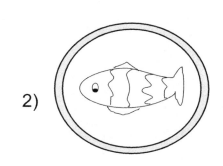

3)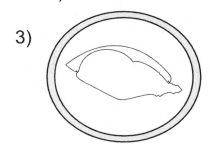

_____

_____

)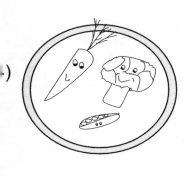

5)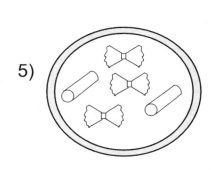

6)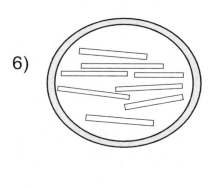

_____

_____

_____

7)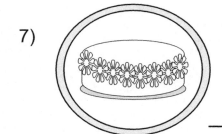

_____

---

 e poulet   le gâteau   le poisson   la viande    les légumes   les pâtes    les pommes frites

Qu'est-ce que tu aimes manger?

(What do you like to eat?)

Salut!

J'aime le poisson et le poulet.

Je n'aime pas la viande.

J'aime le riz mais je préfère les pâtes.

Je n'aime pas la salade.

J'aime les pommes frites.

Salut!

Marc

j'aime ♡
(I like)

et
(and)

je préfère ♡ ♡
(I prefer)

mais
(but)

je n'aime pas
(I don't like) ✖

Lire la lettre de Marc et répondre aux questions:
(Read the letter from Marc and answer the questions)

1) Does Marc like fish? _____Yes_____

2) Does Marc like meat? _____

3) Does Marc like chicken? _____

4) Does Marc prefer rice or pasta? _____

5) Does Marc like salad? _____

6) Does Marc like chips? _____

le poulet

le poisson

la viande

le riz

la salade

les légumes

les pâtes

les pommes frites

Tu aimes les pâtes? (Do you like pasta?)

Tu aimes…?
(Do you like…?)

j'aime
(I like)

je préfère
(I prefer)

je n'aime pas
(I don't like)

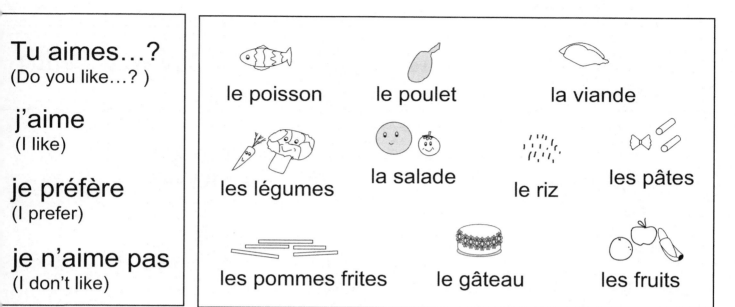

le poisson   le poulet   la viande

les légumes   la salade   le riz   les pâtes

les pommes frites   le gâteau   les fruits

Écrire en français: (Write in French:)

Tu aimes les pâtes?

) Do you like pasta?   ___ _____ ___ _____ .

) Do you like chicken?   ___ _____ ___ _____ .

) Do you like fish?   ___ _____ ___ _____ .

) I like rice   J'aime ___ _____ .

) I like fruit   _____ ___ _____ .

) I like meat   _____ ___ _____ .

) I prefer chips   Je préfère ___ _____ _____ .

) I prefer cake   ___ _____ ___ _____ .

) I don't like salad   Je n'aime pas ___ _____ .

0) I don't like vegetables   ___ _____ ____ ____ _____ .

Qu'est-ce que vous voulez?

(What do you want?)

Je voudrais ….. I would like	avec … with

Sophie

Je voudrais le poulet avec de la salade.

Je voudrais le poisson avec des légumes.

Luc

Marc

Je voudrais la viande avec des pommes frites.

Paul

Je voudrais des pâtes.

Marie

Je voudrais le poulet avec du riz.

Lire les phrases. (Read the sentences.)

Répondre aux questions: (Answer the questions:)

1) Who would like some pasta? _____

2) Who would like chicken with rice? _____

3) What does Luc want? _____ with _____

4) What does Sophie want? _____ with _____

5) What does Marc want? _____ with _____

In French there are 3 ways of saying our word "some":

du

de la

des

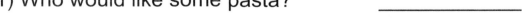

le
poulet

le
poisson

la
viande

du
riz

de la
salade

des
légumes

des
pâtes

des
pommes frites

26

Au restaurant (at the restaurant)

| Je voudrais (I would like) | 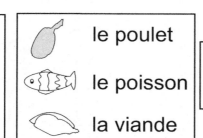 le poulet le poisson la viande | avec (with) |  du riz des pommes frites des pâtes de la salade des légumes |

Écrire en français: (Write in French:)

) I would like the chicken with some rice:

Je voudrais le poulet avec du riz.

_____ .

) I would like the meat with some vegetables:

_____ .

) I would like the fish with some chips:

_____ .

) I would like the chicken with some pasta:

_____ .

) I would like the meat with some rice:

_____ .

) I would like the fish with some salad:

_____ .

) I would like the chicken with some chips:

_____ .

La nourriture (food)

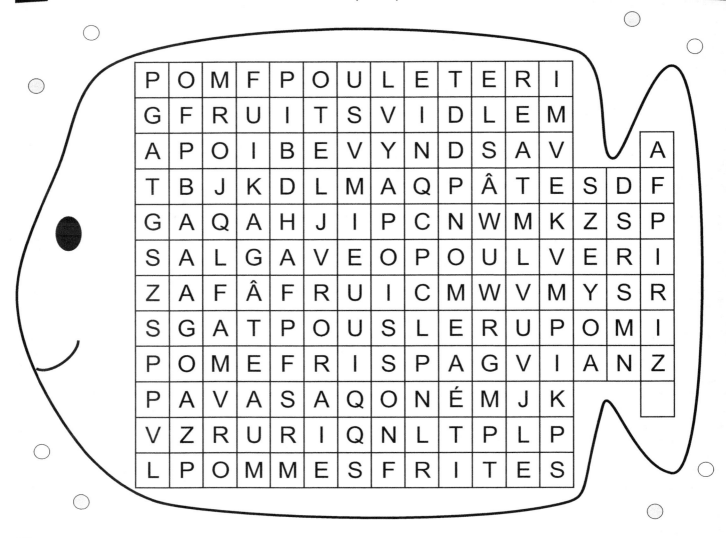

P	O	M	F	P	O	U	L	E	T	E	R	I	
G	F	R	U	I	T	S	V	I	D	L	E	M	
A	P	O	I	B	E	V	Y	N	D	S	A	V	A
T	B	J	K	D	L	M	A	Q	P	Â	T	E	S	D	F
G	A	Q	A	H	J	I	P	C	N	W	M	K	Z	S	P
S	A	L	G	A	V	E	O	P	O	U	L	V	E	R	I
Z	A	F	Â	F	R	U	I	C	M	W	V	M	Y	S	R
S	G	A	T	P	O	U	S	L	E	R	U	P	O	M	I
P	O	M	E	F	R	I	S	P	A	G	V	I	A	N	Z
P	A	V	A	S	A	Q	O	N	É	M	J	K	
V	Z	R	U	R	I	Q	N	L	T	P	L	P	
L	P	O	M	M	E	S	F	R	I	T	E	S	

Trouver ces mots: (Look for these words:)

le POISSON

le POULET

la VIANDE

la SALADE

les FRUITS

les PÂTES

les LÉGUMES

le RIZ

le GÂTEAU

les POMMES FRITES

In French there are four different ways of saying our word "the" : le, l', la, les.
These words do not appear in the word search.

28

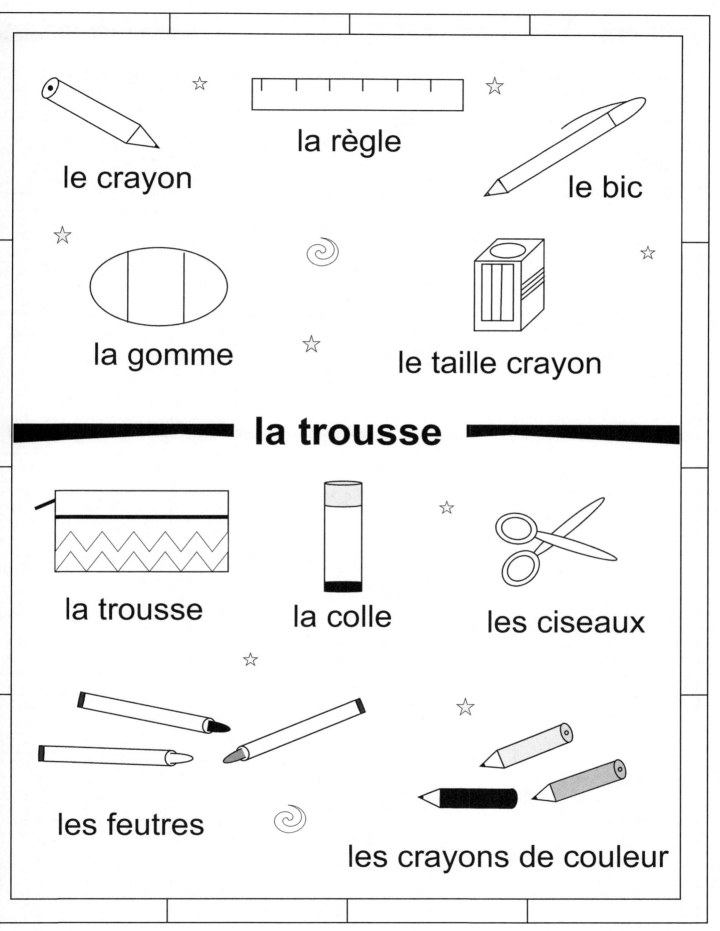

le crayon

la règle

le bic

la gomme

le taille crayon

la trousse

la trousse

la colle

les ciseaux

les feutres

les crayons de couleur

La trousse (the pencil case)

Copier les mots et les dessins: (Copy the words and the pictures:)

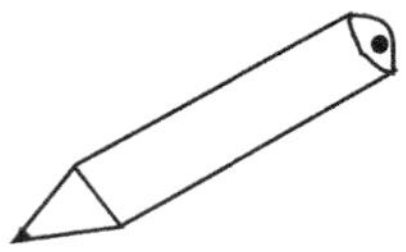

le crayon

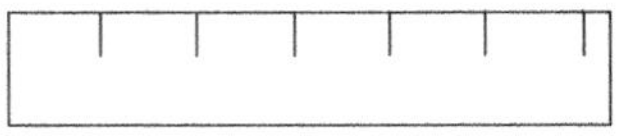

la règle

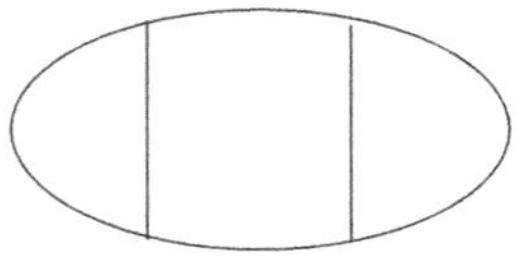

la gomme

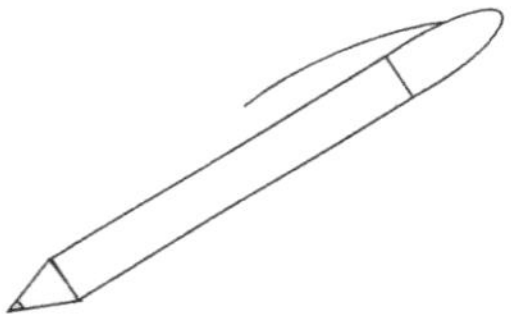

le bic

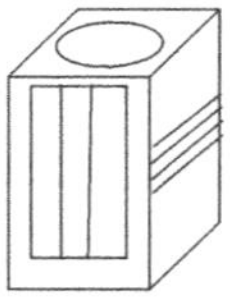

le taille crayon

la colle

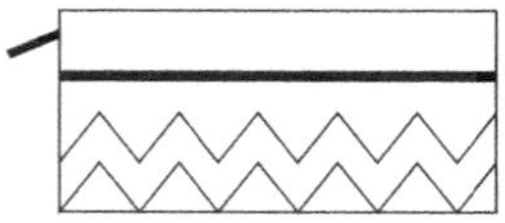

la trousse

C'est de quelle couleur? (What colour is it?)

Colorier les dessins: (Colour the pictures:)

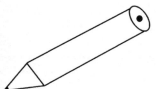

le crayon bleu
(the blue pencil)

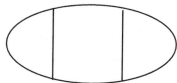

la gomme rouge

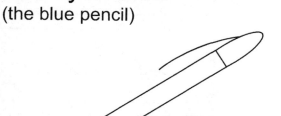

le bic violet

In French the colours go AFTER the noun:
vert ....green
bleu .... blue
rouge ....red
jaune .... yellow
rose .... pink
violet ....purple
marron ...... brown

la règle jaune

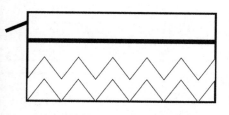

la trousse rouge

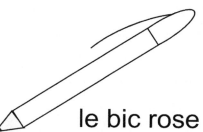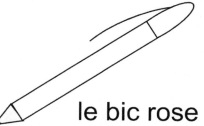

le bic rose

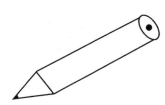

le crayon marron

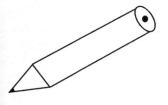

e crayon vert

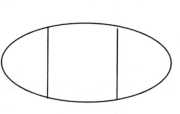

la gomme jaune

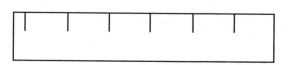

la règle rouge

31

Combien y en a-t-il? (How many are there?)

Relier les boîtes: (Match the boxes:)

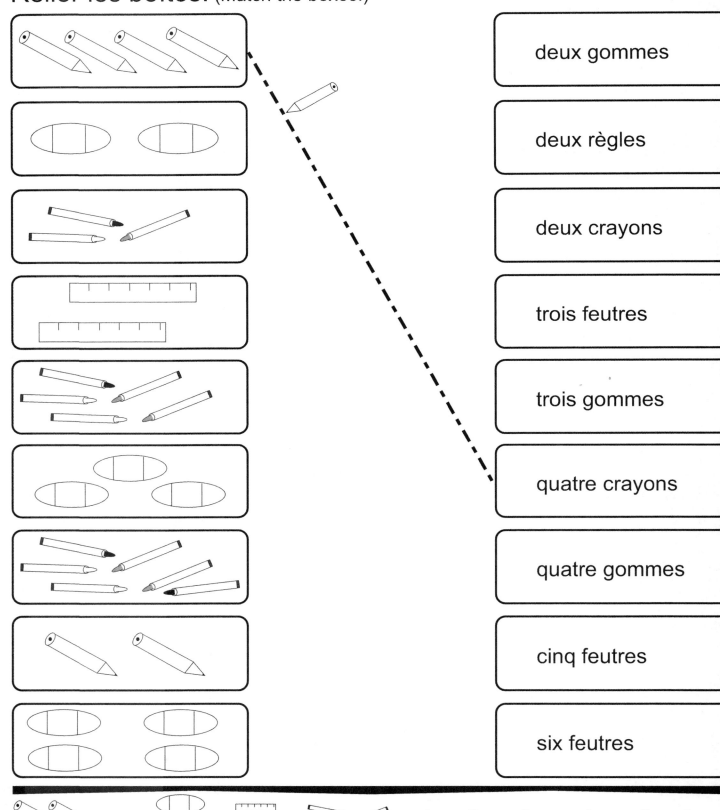

deux gommes

deux règles

deux crayons

trois feutres

trois gommes

quatre crayons

quatre gommes

cinq feutres

six feutres

 crayons

 gommes

 règles

 feutres

1 un   2 deux   3 trois   4 quatre   5 cinq   6 six

Dans ma trousse, j'ai ....

(In my pencil case, I have....)

Salut!

Dans ma trousse j'ai six crayons de couleur, un bic rose, un bic violet et des ciseaux.

Salut!

Anne Marie

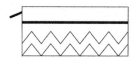

Salut!

Dans ma trousse j'ai un crayon, trois gommes, un bic bleu et une règle rouge.

Salut!

Marc

Salut!

Dans ma trousse j'ai cinq feutres, une gomme rose, un bic vert et une règle rose.

Salut!

Sophie

Lire les cartes. (Read the letters.)

Répondre aux questions: (Answer the questions:)

1) Who has a pink biro and a purple biro?   *Anne-Marie* _____

2) Who has a blue biro and a red ruler?   _____

3) How many felt tips does Sophie have?   _____

4) What colour biro does Sophie have?   _____

5) Who has six colouring pencils?   _____

6) Who has a pink rubber and a pink ruler?   _____

7) Who has a pencil and three rubbers?   _____

n bic	un crayon	une règle	une gomme

vert - green   bleu - blue   rouge - red
rose - pink   violet - purple

des ciseaux

six crayons de couleur

trois gommes

cinq feutres

33

La trousse (the pencil case)

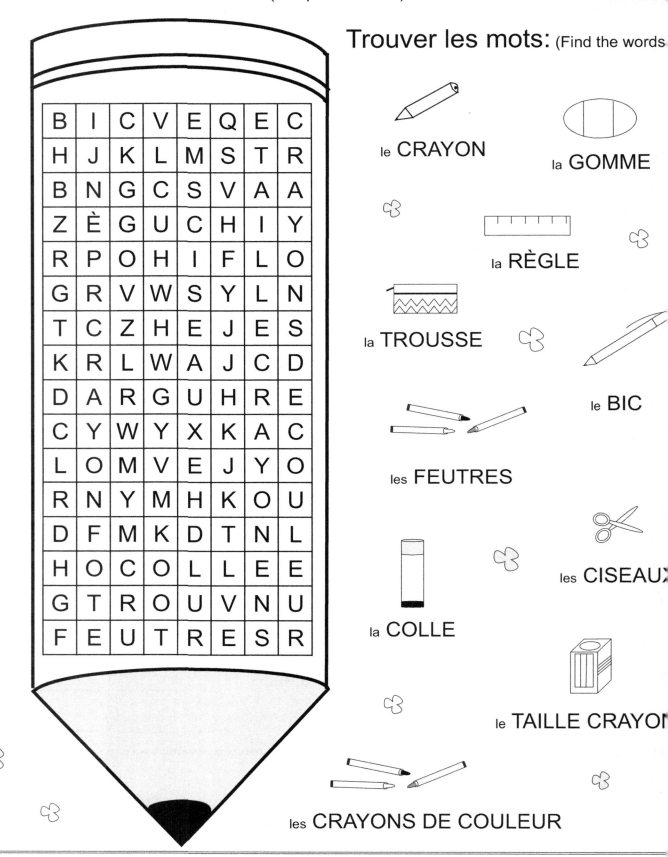

Trouver les mots: (Find the words

B	I	C	V	E	Q	E	C
H	J	K	L	M	S	T	R
B	N	G	C	S	V	A	A
Z	È	G	U	C	H	I	Y
R	P	O	H	I	F	L	O
G	R	V	W	S	Y	L	N
T	C	Z	H	E	J	E	S
K	R	L	W	A	J	C	D
D	A	R	G	U	H	R	E
C	Y	W	Y	X	K	A	C
L	O	M	V	E	J	Y	O
R	N	Y	M	H	K	O	U
D	F	M	K	D	T	N	L
H	O	C	O	L	L	E	E
G	T	R	O	U	V	N	U
F	E	U	T	R	E	S	R

le CRAYON

la GOMME

la RÈGLE

la TROUSSE

le BIC

les FEUTRES

les CISEAUX

la COLLE

le TAILLE CRAYON

les CRAYONS DE COULEUR

In French there are four different ways of saying our word "the" : le, l', la, les.
These words do not appear in the word search.

34

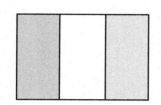

le français

le dessin

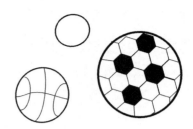

le sport

la religion

la géographie

la musique

Les matières

l'histoire

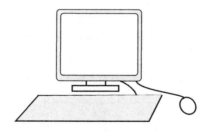

l'informatique

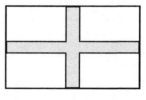

l'anglais

les sciences

$2 + 4 = 6$

les maths

■ Qu'est-ce que c'est? (What is it?)

Regarder les dessins et écrire les mots en français:
(Look at the pictures and write the words in French:)

1) _____

2) _____

3) 2 + 4 = 6
_____

4) _____

5) _____

6) _____

7) _____

8) _____

9) _____

le français   le dessin   le sport   la géographie   la musique   l'histoire   l'anglais   les maths   les science

J'aime le français (I like French)

J'aime ..... I like

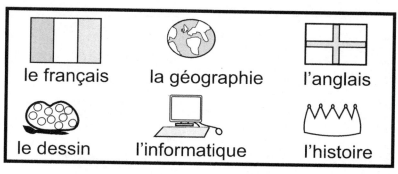

le français   la géographie   l'anglais

le dessin   l'informatique   l'histoire

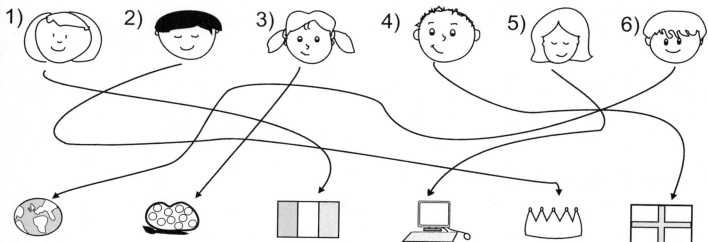

Regarder les dessins et écrire les phrases:
Look at the pictures and sentences:)

J'aime le français,

1) _____ .

2) _____ .

3) _____ .

4) _____ .

5) _____ .

6) _____ .

■ Tu aimes le français? (Do you like French?)

Tu aimes...? (Do you like...?) **j'aime** (I like) **je préfère** (I prefer) **je n'aime pas** (I don't like)	le français ♪♪ ♩ la musique le dessin 〰〰 l'histoire le sport l'anglais la géographie 2 + 4 = 6 les maths l'informatique les sciences

Écrire en français: (Write in French:)

Tu   aimes   le   français?

1) Do you like French?   ___ _____ ___ _____ .

2) Do you like maths?   ___ _____ ___ _____ .

3) Do you like geography?   ___ _____ ___ _____ .

4) I like music   J'aime ___ _____ .

5) I like sport   _____ ___ _____ .

6) I like history   _____ ___ _____ .

7) I prefer I.T.   Je préfère ___ _____ .

8) I prefer art   ___ _____ ___ _____ .

9) I don't like science   Je n'aime pas ___ _____ .

10) I don't like English   ___ _____ ___ _____ .

38

C'est intéressant! (it's interesting)

c'est facile (it's easy)	c'est amusant (it's fun)	c'est utile (it's useful)	c'est intéressant (it's interesting)

Salut!
Le français, c'est utile.
Le sport, c'est amusant.
La géographie, c'est facile.
L'anglais, c'est intéressant.
Salut!

Paul

Salut!
La musique, c'est facile.
Le dessin, c'est amusant.
L'histoire, c'est intéressant.
Les maths, c'est utile.
Salut!

Sophie

Lire les cartes. (Read the letters.)
Répondre aux questions: (Answer the questions:)

Sophie

1) Who finds music easy? _____

2) Who finds French useful? _____

3) Who finds art fun? _____

4) Who finds English interesting? _____

5) What does Paul think of sport? _____

6) What does Sophie think of history? _____

7) What does Paul think of geography? _____

8) What does Sophie think of maths? _____

le français   le dessin   le sport   la géographie   la musique   l'histoire   l'anglais   les maths

Les matières (school subjects)

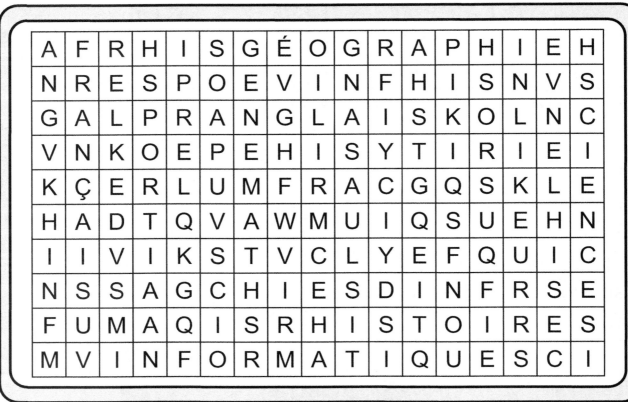

A	F	R	H	I	S	G	É	O	G	R	A	P	H	I	E	H
N	R	E	S	P	O	E	V	I	N	F	H	I	S	N	V	S
G	A	L	P	R	A	N	G	L	A	I	S	K	O	L	N	C
V	N	K	O	E	P	E	H	I	S	Y	T	I	R	I	E	I
K	Ç	E	R	L	U	M	F	R	A	C	G	Q	S	K	L	E
H	A	D	T	Q	V	A	W	M	U	I	Q	S	U	E	H	N
I	I	V	I	K	S	T	V	C	L	Y	E	F	Q	U	I	C
N	S	S	A	G	C	H	I	E	S	D	I	N	F	R	S	E
F	U	M	A	Q	I	S	R	H	I	S	T	O	I	R	E	S
M	V	I	N	F	O	R	M	A	T	I	Q	U	E	S	C	I

Trouver les mots: (Find the words:)

le FRANÇAIS

le DESSIN

la GÉOGRAPHIE

le SPORT

la RELIGION

la MUSIQUE

l' ANGLAIS

l' HISTOIRE

l' INFORMATIQUE

les SCIENCES

les MATHS

In French there are four different ways of saying our word "the" : le, l', la, les.
These words do not appear in the word search.

French	English	French	English
amusant	fun	mais	but
anglais	English	la maison	the house
avec	with	marron	brown
la banque	the bank	les maths	maths
le bic	the biro	les mots	the words
bleu	blue	le musée	the museum
le café	the café	la musique	music
c'est	it's	neuf	nine
la chambre	the bedroom	les numéros	numbers
le chat	the cat	l' oiseau	the bird
le château	the castle	le parc	the park
le chien	the dog	les pâtes	the pasta
cinq	five	petit	small
les ciseaux	the scissors	la piscine	the swimming pool
la colle	the glue	la plage	the beach
colorier	to colour	le poisson	the fish
le crayon	the pencil	les pommes frites	the chips
les crayons de couleur	the colouring pencils	le poulet	the chicken
la cuisine	the kitchen	quatre	four
dans	in	la règle	the ruler
le dessin	art	la religion	R.E.
deux	two	le restaurant	the restaurant
dix	ten	le riz	the rice
facile	easy	rose	pink
les feutres	the felt tip pens	rouge	red
français	French	la salade	the salade
les fruits	the fruit	la salle à manger	the dining room
le gâteau	the cake	la salle de bains	the bathroom
la géographie	geography	le salon	the living room
la gomme	the rubber	les sciences	science
grand	big	sept	seven
histoire	history	le serpent	the snake
l' hôtel	the hotel	six	six
huit	eight	la souris	the mouse
il n'y a pas de	there isn't	le sport	sport
il y a	there is	le supermarché	the supermarket
informatique	I.T.	le taille crayon	the pencil sharpener
intéressant	interesting	trois	three
J'aime	I like	la trousse	the pencil case
le jardin	the garden	Tu aimes ....?	Do you like......?
jaune	yellow	un	one
je n'aime pas	I don't like	utile	useful
je préfère	I prefer	vert	green
je voudrais….	I would like …	la viande	the meat
le lapin	the rabbit	ma ville	my town
les légumes	the vegetables	violet	lilac

1	un
2	deux
3	trois
4	quatre
5	cinq
6	six
7	sept
8	huit
9	neuf
10	dix
11	onze
12	douze
13	treize
14	quatorze
15	quinze
16	seize
17	dix-sept
18	dix-huit
19	dix-neuf
20	vingt
21	vingt-et-un
22	vingt-deux
23	vingt-trois
24	vingt-quatre
25	vingt-cinq
26	vingt-six
27	vingt-sept
28	vingt-huit
29	vingt-neuf
30	trente
31	trente-et-un
32	trente-deux
33	trente-trois
34	trente-quatre
35	trente-cinq
36	trente-six
37	trente-sept
38	trente-huit
39	trente-neuf
40	quarante

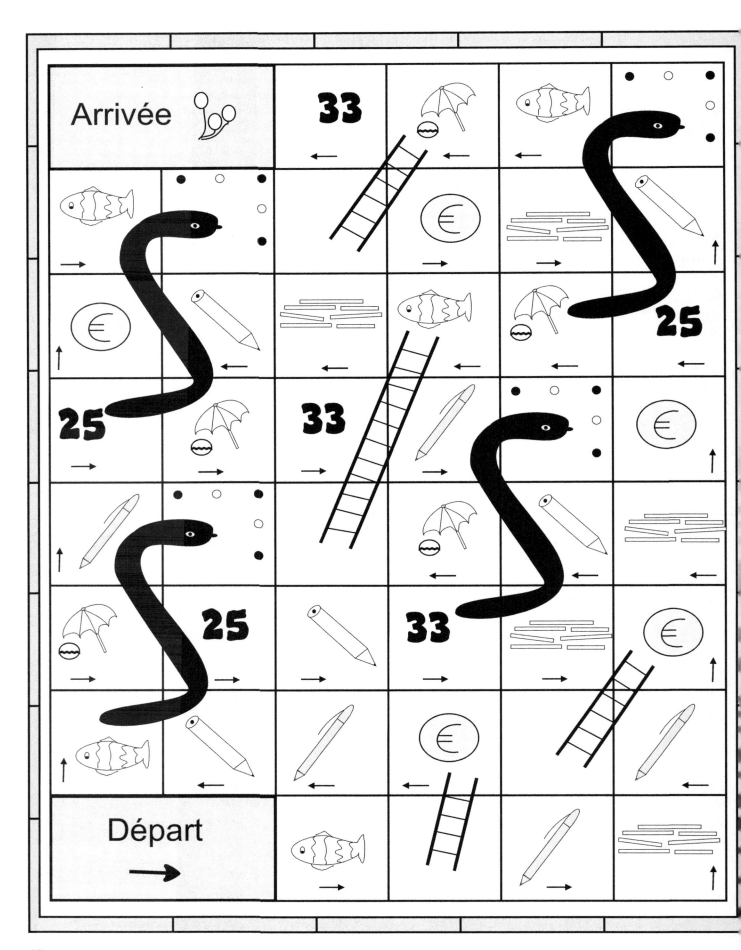

42

Snakes & ladders game

For this game, you will need a dice and a counter for each player. The counters could be rubbers, cubes or you could make your own on pieces of paper.

How to play

Start at "Départ", roll the dice and count that number of squares.

If the final square has the bottom of the ladder in it go up it, or if it has the head of a snake go down it.

Say the word for the picture you land on in French.

Take turns to roll the dice. To win, arrive first at "Arrivée".

Useful French words

la plage
(the beach)

la banque
(the bank)

25
vingt-cinq
(twenty-five)

33
trente-trois
(thirty-three)

le crayon
(the pencil)

le bic
(the biro)

les pommes frites
(the chips)

le poisson
(the fish)

Games are a fun way to learn a foreign language! If you like games you could try the book: French Word Games - Cool Kids Speak French

Answers

Page 2

1) la maison   2) le salon   3) la cuisine   4) la salle à manger   5) le jardin
6) la chambre   7) la salle de bains

Page 3

The picture should be coloured as follows:

The kitchen is red.
The dining room is brown and pink.
The living room is purple.

The bathroom is blue.
The main bedroom is green.
The small bedroom is pink.

Page 4

le jardin	un jardin	la maison	une maison	2a) feminine
le salon	un salon	la cuisine	une cuisine	b) masculine
le garage	un garage	la chambre	une chambre	c) feminine

Page 5

1) la chambre   2) le jardin   3) le garage   4) le salon   5) la cuisine
6) la salle de bains   7) la salle à manger

Page 6

1) B   2) A   3) C
4) A   5) B   6) C

Page 7

S	A	L	L	E	À	M	A	N	G	E	R
C	G	A	R	A	G	E	E				E
H		M				G		N		N	
A	V	A			U		I		I		N
M	E	I		O	D		S		O		B
B	R	S	R		R		I		L		L
R	T	O		A		U		A			E
E		N	J		C		S				U
S	A	L	L	E	D	E	B	A	I	N	S

Page 9

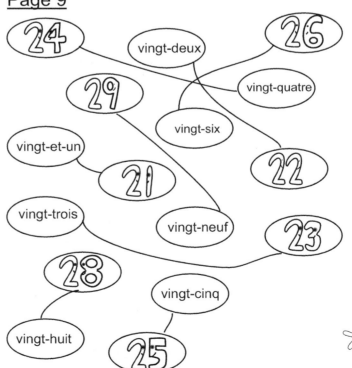

Page 10

a) vingt-sept
b) vingt-quatre
c) vingt-deux
d) vingt-cinq
e) vingt-huit
f) vingt-neuf
g) vingt-et-un
h) trente

44

Page 12

a) trente-deux
b) trente-sept
c) trente-cinq
d) trente-quatre
e) trente-huit
f) quarante
g) trente-et-un
h) trente-neuf

Page 13

a) quatre
b) huit
c) douze
d) quatorze
e) vingt
f) vingt-quatre
g) vingt-huit
h) trente-deux
i) trente-six
j) quarante

Page 14

		V	I	N	G	T	S	E	P	T			
			T	R	E	N	T	E	Q	U	A	T	R	E
T					T	R	E	N	T	E	S	I	X		V
R		T						S		X		Q			I
E		R						I		U		N	V		N
N		E					O		E		I		I		G
T		N			R		D		C		T		N		T
E		T			T		E		T		G		G		N
H		E		T		T		G		N		T			E
U			G		N		N		I			E			U
I												T			F
T		N		E		I		V		D	I	X	T	
	I		R		V							U	
V		T		Q	U	A	R	A	N	T	E		N

Page 16

a) le château
b) la banque
c) le musée
d) le parc
e) le café
f) le restaurant
g) l'hôtel

Page 17

Dans ma ville il y a la plage et la piscine.
Il y a le parc.
Il y a le café et le restaurant.
Il y a le supermarché et la banque.
Il n'y a pas de musée.
Il n'y a pas de château.

Page 18

1) Yes
2) It's big
3) No
4) No
5) It's small
6) Yes
7) No
8) It's small

Page 19

le musée	un musée		la banque	une banque
le restaurant	un restaurant		la plage	une plage
le château	**un** château		la piscine	**une** piscine
le parc	**un** parc			
le café	un café			

2a) a hotel   b) masculine

Page 20

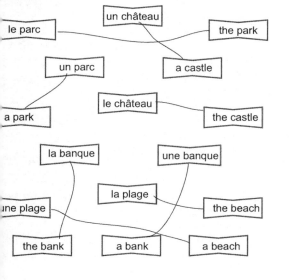

le parc
un château — the park
un parc — a castle
a park
le château — the castle
a park
la banque — une banque
la plage
une plage — the beach
the bank — a bank — a beach

Page 21

		S	U	P	E	R	M	A	R	C	H	É	P		
												A		R
	C	H	Â	T	E	A	U			E		R		E
			L				N			C		S
		E			I					T
	T		E		C		M		A
	Ô		U		S		U		U
H		Q		I		S		R
	N		P		É		A
	A			C	A	F	É	E		N
B								T
	P	L	A	G	E	

45

Page 23

1) le poulet
2) le poisson
3) la viande
4) les légumes
5) les pâtes
6) les pommes frites
7) le gâteau

Page 24

1) Yes
2) No
3) Yes
4) pasta
5) No
6) Yes

Page 25

1) Tu aimes les pâtes?
2) Tu aimes le poulet?
3) Tu aimes le poisson?
4) J'aime le riz.
5) J'aime les fruits.
6) J'aime la viande.
7) Je préfère les pommes frites.
8) Je préfère le gâteau.
9) Je n'aime pas la salade.
10) Je n'aime pas les légumes.

Page 26

1) Paul
2) Marie
3) Fish with vegetables
4) Chicken with salad
5) Meat with chips

Page 27

1) Je voudrais le poulet avec du riz.
2) Je voudrais la viande avec des légumes.
3) Je voudrais le poisson avec des pommes frites.
4) Je voudrais le poulet avec des pâtes.
5) Je voudrais la viande avec du riz.
6) Je voudrais le poisson avec de la salade.
7) Je voudrais le poulet avec des frites.

Page 28

			P	O	U	L	E	T	E		
	F	R	U	I	T	S		D			
				E			N				
			D		A		P	Â	T	E	S	
		A			I	P						S
	L	G		V		O				E		
A		Ã				I			M			R
S		T				S		U				I
		E				S		G				Z
		A				O	É				
		U				N	L				
P	O	M	M	E	S	F	R	I	T	E	S

Page 31

The pictures should be coloured as follows:
le crayon bleu - the blue pencil
la gomme rouge - the red rubber
le bic violet - the purple biro
la règle jaune - the yellow ruler
la trousse rouge - the red pencil case
le bic rose - the pink pen
le crayon marron - the brown pencil
le crayon vert - the green pencil
la gomme jaune - the yellow rubber
la règle rouge - the red ruler

Page 32

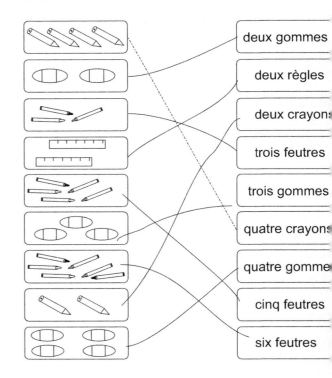

Page 33

) Anne Marie
) Marc
) five
) green
) Anne Marie
) Sophie
) Marc

Page 34

B	I	C		E		E	C
			L		S	T	R
		G		S		A	A
	È		U	C		I	Y
R		O		I		L	O
	R			S		L	N
T	C			E		E	S
	R			A		C	D
	A			U		R	E
	Y			X		A	C
	O			E		Y	O
	N		M			O	U
		M				N	L
	O	C	O	L	L	E	E
G							U
F	E	U	T	R	E	S	R

Page 36

1) le français
2) le sport
3) les maths
4) le dessin
5) l'histoire
6) la musique
7) la géographie
8) l'anglais
9) les sciences

Page 37

1) J'aime le français.
2) J'aime l'histoire.
3) J'aime le dessin.
4) J'aime l'anglais.
5) J'aime l'informatique.
6) J'aime la géographie.

Page 38

) Tu aimes le français?
) Tu aimes les maths?
) Tu aimes la géographie?
) J'aime la musique.
) J'aime le sport.
) J'aime l'histoire.
) Je préfère l'informatique.
) Je préfère le dessin.
) Je n'aime pas les sciences.
0) Je n'aime pas l'anglais.

Page 39

1) Sophie
2) Paul
3) Sophie
4) Paul
5) It's fun
6) It's interesting
7) It's easy
8) It's useful

Page 40

M	F				G	É	O	G	R	A	P	H	I	E	
R		S									N			S
A		P	A	N	G	L	A	I	S		O		N	C
N		O			E				I		I		I	
Ç		R	U	M				G		S			E	
A		T	Q		A		I		S				N	
I		I			T		L		E				C	
S	S				H	E		D					E	
U					S	R	H	I	S	T	O	I	R	E	S
M		I	N	F	O	R	M	A	T	I	Q	U	E	

For children learning French there are also the following books by Joanne Leyland:

On Holiday In France
Cool Kids Speak French

Ideal for holidays and to challenge children to speak French whilst away. Topics include greetings, numbers, drinks, food, souvenirs, town, hotels & campsites.

40 French Word Searches
Cool Kids Speak French

The word searches appear in fun shapes and pictures accompany the French words so that each word search can be a meaningful learning activity. 40 Topics.

French Word Games

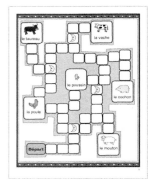

Have fun learning French with this lovely collection of games. The 15 topics include the body, the farm, fruit, the park, the picnic, town, weather, transport...

French At Christmas Time

Bursting with fun Christmas themed activity pages, word searches, colour by number, board games and Christmas cards to make. Photocopiable for class or home use.

Photocopiable Games For Teaching French

Differentiated activities for children of various abilities. The games are colour coded according to the amount of French words in each game.

Games include:
- board games
- Dominoes
- snakes and ladders
- 3 or 4 in a row
- co-ordinates
- mini cards

Topics include:
- Pets
- Colours
- Numbers
- Fruit
- Drinks
- Food
- Clothes
- Sport

Cool Kids Do Maths In French

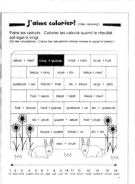

Topics include

- Numbers 1 - 10
- Numbers 11 - 20
- Numbers 21 - 40
- Numbers 41 - 60
- Numbers 60 - 80
- Numbers 80 - 100
- Fractions

A fantastic way for children to learn 1 to 100 in French. Great cross curricular resource. May be photocopied.

Un Alien Sur La Terre

An alien visiting Earth is curious why there are so many things.
Topics: General conversation, clothes, weather, activities.

Le Singe Qui Change De Couleur

A monkey changes colour when he eats. Will he ever return to his usual colour?
Topics: General conversation, days, colours, food, opinions.

Tu As Un Animal?

Marc doesn't have a pet. Will his wish for a pet come true?
Topics: Types of pets, colours, sizes, names of pets, opinions.

First 100 Words In French Coloring Book - Cool Kids Speak French

The 100 French words in this brilliant book include a marvellous mix of favourite children's characters (for example a fairy, a dragon, a mermaid, a dinosaur or a unicorn) and useful French words like some food, types of transport, animals, toys and clothes. The 30 delightful pages all have borders and are single sided.

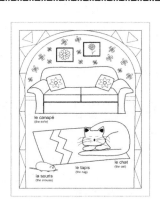

French

Young Cool Kids Learn French
French Colouring Book For Kids Ages 5 - 7
First Words In French Teacher's Resource Book
Stories for 3-7 year olds: Jack And The French Languasaurus - Books 1, 2 & 3,
Daniel And The French Robot - Books 1, 2 & 3, Sophie And The French Magician
Cool Kids Speak French - Books 1, 2 & 3 *(for kids ages 7 - 11)*
French Word Games - Cool Kids Speak French
Photocopiable Games For Teaching French
40 French Word Searches Cool Kids Speak French
First 100 Words In French Coloring Book Cool Kids Speak French
French at Christmas time
On Holiday In France Cool Kids Speak French
Cool Kids Do Maths In French
Stories in French: Un Alien Sur La Terre, Le Singe Qui Change De Couleur, Tu As Un Animal?

Italian

Young Cool Kids Learn Italian
Italian Colouring Book For Kids Ages 5 - 7
Cool Kids Speak Italian - Books 1, 2 & 3 *(for kids ages 7 - 11)*
Italian Word Games - Cool Kids Speak Italian
Photocopiable Games For Teaching Italian
40 Italian Word Searches Cool Kids Speak Italian
First 100 Words In Italian Coloring Book Cool Kids Speak Italian
On Holiday In Italy Cool Kids Speak Italian
Stories in Italian: Un Alieno Sulla Terra, La Scimmia Che Cambia Colore, Hai Un Animale Domestico

German

Young Cool Kids Learn German
German Colouring Book For Kids Ages 5 - 7
Sophie And The German Magician *(a story for 3-7 year olds)*
Cool Kids Speak German - Books 1, 2 & 3 *(for kids ages 7 - 11)*
German Word Games - Cool Kids Speak German
Photocopiable Games For Teaching German
40 German Word Searches Cool Kids Speak German
First 100 Words In German Coloring Book Cool Kids Speak German

Spanish

Young Cool Kids Learn Spanish
Spanish Colouring Book For Kids Ages 5 - 7
First Words In Spanish Teacher's Resource Book
Stories for 3-7 year olds: Jack And The Spanish Dinosaur, Sophie And The Spanish Magician,
Daniel And The Spanish Robot - Books 1, 2 & 3
Cool Kids Speak Spanish - Books 1, 2 & 3 *(for kids ages 7 - 11)*
Spanish Word Games - Cool Kids Speak Spanish
Photocopiable Games For Teaching Spanish
40 Spanish Word Searches Cool Kids Speak Spanish
First 100 Words In Spanish Coloring Book Cool Kids Speak Spanish
Spanish at Christmas time
On Holiday In Spain Cool Kids Speak Spanish
Cool Kids Do Maths In Spanish
Stories in Spanish: Un Extraterrestre En La Tierra, El Mono Que Cambia De Color, Seis Mascotas

English as a second language / foreign language

English For Kids Ages 5 - 7
English Colouring Book For Kids Ages 5 - 7
Cool Kids Speak English - Books 1, 2 & 3 *(for kids ages 7 - 11)*
First Words In English - 100 Words To Colour & Learn
English Word Games
Fun Word Search Puzzles

Printed in Great Britain
by Amazon

27811932R00031